$\mathcal{B}$ELIEVE

Original Paintings by N.A. Noël
Original Poetry by John Wm. Sisson

Do you believe?
Then tell me...

Have you heard an angel pray,
Perhaps for love and grace?
What would an angel have to say
In such a heavenly place?

What words of joy and those of praise
Would angels give a voice?
When speaking of warm summer days,
What words would be their choice?

And flowers in the early spring
On hill or forest lawn,
What would a heavenly angel sing
To greet them every dawn?

Or maybe on a mountain top
Or in a valley wide,
Or any place that makes you stop
Where angels play and hide.

One wonders of the words they'd use,
What songs would they inspire?
Which poems would the angels choose
From an angel heart's desire?

Wisdom

Wisdom is an angel friend you'll find
When you explore,
Through knowledge and experience
What lies behind life's door.

Wisdom leads you from the darkness
Moving toward the light,
By teaching you to find the wrong
And turn it into right.

Wisdom moves with generations
Father to the Son,
A cycle of renewal
Making Mother, Daughter one.

With Wisdom comes enlightenment
Of who we really are,
Living beings on a planet
Circling 'round a star.

Wisdom with her nature's crown
Will light upon your being,
The flowering of her glory
So much more than we are seeing.

For each of us to everyone just like
A simple flower,
Becomes a living sample of the
Beauty of God's power.

Wisdom's universal song for
Humankind is true,
You must do unto others what you
Wish done unto you.

Peace & Harmony

Here are two that are so close
They always stay in tune;
How could we have the shining sun
Without the silvery moon?

The only way that you'll find Peace
Is finding Harmony,
And when you find the two of them
They both will set you free.

Just sit there still with Harmony
And close your eyes with Peace,
And soon you'll feel an inner strength
From a source that will not cease.

It's when there's Peace and Harmony
That all of us can grow;
Beyond those of our wildest dreams,
Beyond yet what we know.

Side by side and on through time
Go Peace and Harmony,
And trust me when you find the one
There will the other be.

Faith

Here we are with little Faith
A giant without measure,
It's those who keep a little Faith
Who always find life's treasure.

A little Faith will guide us on
Through darkest hour of night,
While others may not see the dawn
We'll see her morning light.

Who knows, with just a little Faith
And all her angel's charm
We'll make our mother planet safe,
All creatures safe from harm.

From flowers in the fertile fields
To mountains fresh with snow,
Abundance from God's bounty yields
The fruits that make Faith grow.

So you can see with love and grace
And even joy unbound,
It's good to keep about the place
A little Faith around.

Humility

Everyday with Humility
We always make our way,
She gives us the ability
To humble what we say.

We always seek her tender eyes
When cast in our direction,
We're humbled as we realize
The depth of her affection.

Humility sits there with grace
She waits upon the faithful,
And humbly she sets a place
For even those ungrateful.

Humility with charity
An honored way to give,
A gift from your sincerity
That helps another live.

Humility in all we do
Though through this life we stumble,
In every age they always knew
That God rewards the humble.

Love

Of all the angels high above
There's one above the rest.
Of course this angel's name is Love
Among us all most blest.

Love's in the air caressing spring
With every passing breeze.
Love's in the warmth that summer brings,
Love's in the autumn leaves.

Love's in the souls that are so pure
Who seek for God's salvation;
He helps their spirits to endure
Through faith and adoration.

Love's in the causes won and lost
For Love is in the labor.
We all forget the trials crossed
When seeking Love's sweet favor.

Love guides our angel's every move
Which isn't all that odd.
How could we work or scarce improve
Without the Love of God?

Charity

There's one who speaks with clarity
And gentleness of mind.
We love our friend sweet Charity
For acts she does divine.

Yes, Charity can feed the poor;
She helps the sick and tired.
Those brought low before her door
Leave fresh, renewed, inspired.

An act to lend a helping hand
To a stranger or a neighbor,
Will resonate throughout the land
And always win God's favor.

That's the part in all our minds
That seems the most sincere,
The joy of giving each one finds
With Charity each year.

Hope

It's Hope that's there when you're in need
To somewhere, somehow plant the seed
That yes, there's Hope to carry on;
Support the weak and make them strong.

Whatever contest may be held
Or when it seems your cause be felled,
When all seems lost and without reason
Hope springs alive; she'll have her season.

That little seed from long ago
She planted there will start to grow,
Because of Hope we'll all survive
Because we all kept Hope alive.

That seed she nestled in our breast
That helps make us our very best,
An angel's gift she loves to share
You'll always know that Hope is there.

Miracle

Do you believe in Miracles?
Well all the angels do,
If you knew our friend Miracle
Then you'd believe them too.

The miracles that she performs
Delight us through the ages,
From magic to the unicorns
To wisdom from the sages.

The Miracle of faith is one,
Friendship is another,
The Golden Rule, the golden sun,
A baby with its Mother.

Why Miracles are everywhere,
They're in a child's eyes,
A tree, a leaf beyond compare,
The colors in the skies.

The Miracle of planet earth
We're told by all our teachers,
Is way beyond a scale of worth
When weighing all God's creatures.

The greatest gift they say of all
Through laughter, joy and strife,
All God's angels simply call,
The Miracle of life.

Grace

Here's the one with such a face
That all of us will seek for Grace,
So full of charm with virtue mild
This gift to us this graceful child.

You always know when Grace takes wing,
The sun will shine, the birds will sing;
And everywhere in every place
The world will seem so full of Grace.

By Grace of God we use our time
To contemplate these things divine;
And when we take our slumber here,
We have no doubt or even fear
That Grace of God will guide us on,
Protect our night from dusk to dawn,
And every morn her wish will be,
We'll rise anew so gracefully.

And when the day is nearly done,
With each success that you have won,
It's then God's angels sing with glee,
We're glad to grant our Grace to thee.

Compassion

Compassion is an angel
Who always gives her all,
She's there for every creature
Whether great or whether small.

At any time of day or night
Or any kind of storm,
She'll wrap her arms around your soul
To keep you safe and warm.

Compassion swells within a heart
When someone is in pain,
It softly beats a rhythm
So gentle and humane.

No matter if it's man or beast
Or what their tale of woe,
Compassion with her wings outstretched
Will help the healing grow.

Compassion has a kindness
Seen in every tender act.
So when you're kind to someone else
I tell you it's a fact...
Sometime she'll be around again
For all the angels say,
Compassion shown to others
Will be shown to you someday.

To my sons, Alexander and Michael...
*who taught me to **Believe**.*

– N.A. NOËL

❧

To my Grandmother, my Mother, my Sister
and Nancy Noël for their encouragement, love and
dedication to God.

– JOHN WM. SISSON

*O*ur prayer for you

Angels are a gift to us,
They come from God above.
You'll feel them all about you,
When you live your life with love.

As the seasons take their turn
We hope with joy and care,
It is our wish you'll feel the bliss
Of all the angels there.

We hope you find the magic
And the wisdom of the wise,
Who knew that everything they saw
Could not be seen with eyes.

So with a humble spirit
We hope that this will fill,
A spot deep within your heart
With solitude so still.

You'll know that this angelic art
And this poetic rhyme
Is made for you and yes it's true,
For you throughout all time.

Please let this be our prayer for you
That every single day,
You feel angels everywhere
In all you do and say.

No matter whether clouds are gray
Or skies of crystal blue,
You'll always know that with our love
We send this book to you…

John

Some of the original paintings in this book are also available as open edition fine art prints.
For information on purchasing prints and award-winning books, or to request a free full-color NOËL STUDIO catalog:
1-800-444-6635
www.nanoël.com

Copyright © 1997 NOËL STUDIO, Inc.
5618 West 73rd Street
Indianapolis, IN 46278

Cover design by Betsy Knotts
Editing by A.A. Nolfo-Wheeler

Library of Congress Catalog Card Number: 97-069537
ISBN 0-9652531-1-2

*B*elieve features a glow in the dark cover...
Limited gold edition also available.